Work.
Life.

Work.
Life.

Lessons from leaders

CLAIRE O'CONNELL

Acadamh Ríoga na hÉireann
Royal Irish Academy

Work. Life. Lessons from leaders

First published 2023
Royal Irish Academy, 19 Dawson Street, Dublin 2
ria.ie

British Library Cataloguing in Publication Data. A CIP catalogue record for this book is available from the British Library.

ISBN 978-1-911479-77-2 (PB)
ISBN 978-1-911479-93-2 (pdf)
ISBN 978-1-911479-96-3 (epub)

This publication has received support from **accenture**

Editor: Helena King
Book design: Fidelma Slattery
Printed in Ireland by Walsh Colour Print

Royal Irish Academy is a member of Publishing Ireland,
the Irish book publishers' association

5 4 3 2 1

FSC
www.fsc.org
MIX
Paper from
responsible sources
FSC® C165815

A NOTE FROM THE PUBLISHER
We want to try to offset the environmental impacts of carbon produced during the production of our books and journals. For the production of our books this year we will plant 45 trees with Easy Treesie.

Introduction

There is no better teacher than experience. In its absence, we can learn from the experience of others. That is what this book is about.

It's a collection of short snippets of hard-earned wisdom and insights from people—mostly women—who have achieved much in their careers.

The advice you will find here is, for the most part, distilled from a series of masterclasses run by the Royal Irish Academy and Accenture Ireland.

The format of each masterclass was simple: a reputed leader in a particular field met with ten to fifteen participants and, over the course of a few hours, described how they forged their career path, recalled challenging moments and answered questions that sparked discussions about life, work, overcoming barriers and paving the way to success.

What these individuals have learned may provide valuable insights for you; whether it's tips on finding a mentor, getting into a productive mindset or keeping a balance between the demands of work and home. Their advice is often simple too, as many powerful things are.

Dip in and savour the pearls of wisdom found in these pages. Some insights may resonate now, others may chime at a later point in your life or career and provoke you to push barriers. Tuck them away for the journey. See them as arrows in your quiver, or as nuggets of wisdom to pass on in turn.

Contributors

Zahra Bahrololoumi • Michaela Blott • Geraldine
Byrne Nason • Linda Doyle • Frances Fitzgerald
Silvia Giordani • Mary Harney • Barbara Harvey
Mary Kelly • Rose Anne Kenny • Brian MacCraith
Rhona Mahony • Jane Ohlmeyer • Orlaigh Quinn
Louise Richardson • Frances Ruane • Margaret
Sweeney • Sinéad Walsh

Make time for exercise at the start of the day

Professor Rose Anne Kenny is an expert on how to live a long and healthy life. As the principal investigator on the Irish Longitudinal Study on Ageing (TILDA) she has overseen one of the largest studies of this kind in the world: tracking the health of individuals aged 50 and over as they age. Rose Anne's research shows that making time to exercise part of your morning routine will give you more energy to tackle the day ahead. She tries to invest in her own health by taking regular cold showers, weekend cold-water swimming and incorporating movement first thing each day. Her experience of the benefits is such that even after breaking her leg, she continued a morning routine of exercising her muscles with weights while seated.

Value people, nurture talent and keep listening

Physicist Professor Brian MacCraith learned valuable lessons about leadership while serving as president of Dublin City University from 2010 to 2020. One of his key insights is to surround yourself with people who can challenge you, and be proactive about nurturing and acknowledging talent. Tell people they are valued; write and congratulate them on their accomplishments. As a leader, it's important not to distance yourself from the conversations that take place in and about your organisation. Brian advises making it a priority to schedule meetings with colleagues from across your organisation.

Suppress the need to be perfect when balancing your professional and personal life

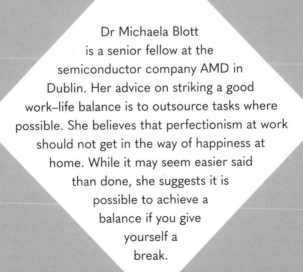

Dr Michaela Blott
is a senior fellow at the
semiconductor company AMD in
Dublin. Her advice on striking a good
work–life balance is to outsource tasks where
possible. She believes that perfectionism at work
should not get in the way of happiness at
home. While it may seem easier said
than done, she suggests it is
possible to achieve a
balance if you give
yourself a
break.

Stop saying
you are just lucky;

start saying
you are good

One of the best pieces of advice that Professor Silvia Giordani received as a young chemistry student in Italy was to acknowledge that it wasn't luck but her own talent, abilities and hard work that resulted in her success. Initially she was shocked at this idea, but over time she realised that this mindset builds your confidence and allows you to be grateful for the people and circumstances that have supported you, but also to recognise that your own talent and abilities are a large part of your success. Today, Silvia is professor of nanomaterials and head of the School of Chemical Sciences at Dublin City University.

Be compassionate with others— and yourself

Barbara Harvey's work as a research manager at Accenture focused on diversity, inclusion and mental health. She is keenly aware of the need to be kind and compassionate with colleagues, because you never know what others are dealing with. Although she is generally in favour of taking on tasks that can stretch you—we learn more from challenging tasks than easy ones and stress in small doses can prove motivating and have a positive effect—Barbara emphasises the need to balance this with practising self-care. This includes being compassionate with yourself and avoiding taking too much on.

**Be pragmatic
about reaching goals:
forge ahead;
say 'no' wisely;
let others in**

Professor Jane Ohlmeyer has led numerous initiatives at Trinity College Dublin, not least the establishment of the Trinity Long Room Hub, a centre for cultural and historical study. Her advice is if you have an idea, act on it. Don't wait for approval from others. Forge ahead with making it happen. Stay focused. Say no to the invitations or tasks that will be counter-productive to reaching your goals. Jane also recommends being open to letting others help you achieve your objectives. This may mean occasionally letting someone else take your idea forward. You can ensure your role in initiating a project is acknowledged and credited at a later stage, perhaps by thanking everyone who worked on bringing your idea to fruition.

When the door opens, go in

In 1977, at the age of 24, Mary Harney became the youngest ever member of Seanad Éireann. At this time, women were very much in the minority in the Oireachtas—the women's room in Leinster House was tucked under the stairs, with a sink, a couch and a desk. Mary was aware that her youth was conspicuous. When first elected to Dáil Éireann in 1981, she was advised that as a young deputy she would do well if she kept her mouth shut. Instead, she seized opportunities and spoke up. Since then, she forged a long and distinguished career in politics and held several ministerial positions. Her many other accomplishments include being one of the founding members, and subsequently leader, of the Progressive Democrats party and becoming Ireland's first female tánaiste.

You may be part of the problem— be open to that

When obstetrician Dr Rhona Mahony became Master of the National Maternity Hospital at Holles Street in Dublin, she was the first woman to hold such a position at a maternity hospital in Ireland. She advises that when difficult or sensitive conversations need to be had with team members, it helps to have prepared the scaffolding for such conversations in advance. Understanding the context and the facts is important, as is recognising that you may be part of the problem. If so, Rhona advises taking the course of action that is in the best interest of the team, rather than simply doing what is best for you.

When faced with a new situation, challenge or opportunity, look for the familiar and hold on to that as you learn

Dr Sinéad Walsh has faced plenty of challenges throughout her career to date. She worked with Concern and Irish Aid at the border between Afghanistan and Pakistan and served as Ireland's first ambassador to Sierra Leone and Liberia. She directs the first Climate Unit to be set up at Ireland's Department of Foreign Affairs. Sinéad has approached each new role by tapping into those aspects of the work—be it places, people or previous expertise—that are familiar. The reassurance of the familiar helps you quickly add value to those elements of the role while you build the new skills required for undertaking the rest of the job, and prevents the challenge of the newness from becoming overwhelming.

Find what you like to do; tackle the jobs others avoid

Prior to becoming Executive Vice President and CEO of Salesforce UK and Ireland, Zahra Bahrololoumi was Senior Managing Director and lead of Accenture Technology for the UK and Ireland. She did not have a technical background when she started at Accenture and instead developed her understanding of technology by learning from others. She built her reputation by proactively resolving issues that others were reluctant to deal with. Over time, this led to Zahra being offered more difficult challenges and, in turn, more senior leadership roles.

Get off the island! Develop perspective. Step back from work occasionally

Professor Frances Ruane is honorary professor of economics at Trinity College Dublin and former director of the Economic and Social Research Institute. Her advice is to periodically apply yourself to developing a new skill and build on your areas of expertise. Frances suggests taking time out between roles if you are moving to a new position, and perhaps do some training. Learning a new skill helps develop a fresh perspective on your work.

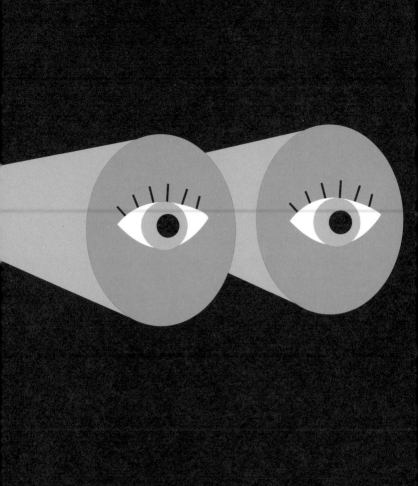

Have the courage to forge your own path

Dr Mary Kelly has had an unusual career path. Having trained as a chemist, she left the pharmaceutical industry to focus on her family. While listening to her kitchen radio and wondering if that was all there is to life, she decided to change direction and studied for an MBA. Her mix of studies combined with her interests and skills saw her achieve environmental leadership roles at the Irish Business and Employers Confederation (Ibec) and the Environmental Protection Agency (where she became director general), and she went on to chair An Bord Pleanála. Mary's advice is to find good mentors and, when you see a role or project of interest, draw on your own integrity and values and have the courage to go for it.

Seize opportunities. Success is the best revenge

Professor Louise Richardson describes herself as hanging on by her fingernails as a young woman juggling a career in academic leadership with the needs of her young family. As a junior academic in Harvard, she occasionally found herself stashing her toddler under the table at weekly departmental meetings that took place after the campus childcare facility closed for the day. Louise's advice is to amass as many experiences as you can; to be forward about building your network; and not to wallow in difficulties or in the face of insults. Instead, seize opportunities to get ahead: success is the best revenge! Louise is the first female vice-chancellor of Oxford University.

If you don't know where to start, start with something simple

When Professor Silvia Giordani, a chemist, moved to work in a physics laboratory she felt out of her depth and was unsure how she could contribute. On the advice of her father, she looked for something small on which she might be able to make a difference. Silvia noticed the lab was using a chemical solvent that wasn't suited to the task at hand. She initiated a project to test other solvents. This led to a much more efficient protocol being developed and published. It is now widely used by researchers in the field.

You will reach a level where you can't do everything. Perfect the basics, learn to skate across the top, and surround yourself with experts

Dr Orlaigh Quinn started her career as a clerical assistant in the Department of Posts and Telegraphs and worked her way up in the Civil Service to become Ireland's eighth female departmental secretary-general. Orlaigh's tips for success include listening carefully to people when you begin a new role, developing an overview of the fundamentals of the job and surrounding yourself with a strong team of people with specific knowledge to whom you can delegate.

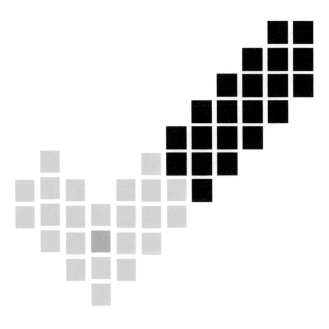

Get into the room where it happens

Geraldine Byrne Nason is Ambassador of Ireland to the United States of America and prior to that was the permanent representative of Ireland to the United Nations in New York. She led Ireland's successful bid for a seat on the UN Security Council for 2021–2 and previously served as second secretary-general in the Department of An Taoiseach, becoming the highest-ranking female public servant in Ireland. Geraldine suggests that climbing the ranks can sometimes involve volunteering for the less glamorous tasks. She advises that grasping opportunities, such as note taking in the room where important discussions are held, can give you an insider's view into how processes work and decisions are made. The opportunities that arise can be invaluable.

Focus on excellence,

Politician Mary Harney introduced numerous policy changes that have had long-lasting impact on Irish life. These include overseeing the founding of the Environmental Protection Agency, the establishing of the independent Personal Injuries Assessment Board, working on the reform of cancer care, and banning smoky

not convenience

coal in Dublin—a move that reduced smog and
saved thousands of lives. It wasn't always easy,
and Mary's advice is, when faced with opposition
from vested interests, to concentrate on what is
in the public's best interest; focus on excellence,
not convenience.

Reframe imposter syndrome: feeling out of your depth can be a positive sign

In 2021, Professor Linda Doyle became the first female Provost of Trinity College Dublin in the institution's 429-year history. Linda suggests that imposter syndrome—the sense that you haven't earned your achievements and are not meant to be in the position you have—is something many people experience when faced with uncertainty. Her advice is to reframe this as a positive feeling that comes with embracing new challenges and stepping out of your comfort zone.

Take side-steps to enrich your career and perspective

Ambassador Geraldine Byrne Nason's advice on developing your career is to look at it in blocks or modules. Take risks, such as side-steps into other paths along the way. Diverging from the conventional career path can offer new experiences that can be useful in building your leadership skills. For Geraldine, taking a post at the OECD, outside the 'classical' diplomatic track, gave her a more international and independent perspective on Ireland. This has served her well, particularly in her role at the United Nations.

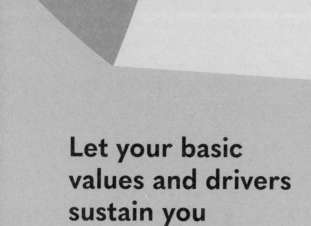

Let your basic values and drivers sustain you

Frances Fitzgerald, MEP for Dublin, has had a prominent career in politics (including as tánaiste), with a particular focus on equality and social issues. Frances is struck by how her experience as a student followed by 20 years as a social-work professional informed her values and actions when she served in politics, most notably as Minister for Justice and Equality. She says that knowing your basic values and drivers is incredibly sustaining in the ups and downs of a career in politics; it is important to follow what motivates you and to love what you do.

Learn to
be a good
listener

As an introvert, Barbara Harvey used to struggle with attending work-related meetings and networking events. She often wanted to hide in a corner or leave events that were a central part of her work at the Gas Consumers' Council, *Which?* magazine and Accenture. Barbara overcame these inhibitions by learning how to listen and engage well: sit forward in meetings and make eye contact to build engagement while listening. She also advises preparing three constructive potential 'everyday' conversations in advance of meeting people, to help break the ice and encourage conversation.

Mind your mindset

Success is not always linear.
It is a continuum, and sometimes success is getting to do the things that satisfy you and that you enjoy.

— Mary Harney

It is important to carve out a place and time to think and focus. Even when you are in the thick of a situation, take a moment to step back from the frenzy and work out what it is you want from that situation.

— Frances Fitzgerald

Avoid falling into a mindset of victimhood when managing challenges in work or your personal life. Instead, see them as an opportunity to build resilience.

— Louise Richardson

You will likely learn a lot about yourself when faced with difficult situations. While it may not be apparent at the time, you may come to benefit from those situations at a later stage.

— Sinéad Walsh

Humour can defuse a tense situation. It buys you time to revisit the difficult topic when you have planned an appropriate response.

— Michaela Blott

If you are tired or in a bad mood, park it. Don't let your mood have a negative effect on others in the room.

— Orlaigh Quinn

Make meetings meaningful

Work with colleagues in advance to ensure that goals are achieved.

— Jane Ohlmeyer

Prepare ahead of tackling a sensitive meeting or topic.

— Rhona Mahony

Speak up and take chances.
Ask for support in advance of an important meeting or make suggestions ahead of time about what you could do to get things rolling. Have your facts and figures ready to support your argument. Ask yourself what is the worst that can happen—it's probably not that bad!

— Linda Doyle

Power is taken, not given.

Summon the courage to raise your hand in meetings and make yourself heard. Instead of dwelling on who is going to let you in, ask what is going to stop you.

— Geraldine Byrne Nason

You can care too much about what others say.

Don't underestimate what can be achieved by drawing on your own integrity and not being swayed by the opinions of others.

— Mary Kelly

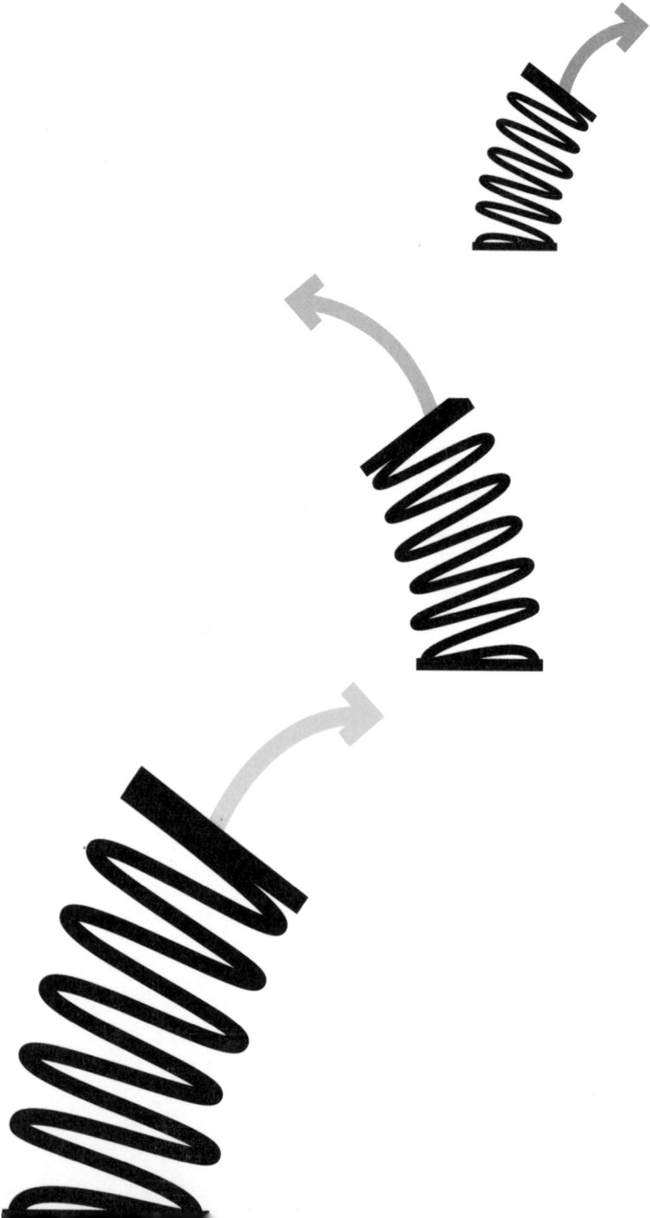

Marvellous mentors

FIND ONE

**Your mentors
can be your peers.**

— Mary Kelly

**The strongest mentorship
relationships are where
the successes of both
sides are linked.**

— Zahra Bahrololoumi

**Seek out more support
and mentorship** as you assume
greater responsibilities.

— Frances Fitzgerald

**It is a strength, not a
weakness, to ask for
help and guidance.**

— Silvia Giordani

BE ONE

You can lift others by spotting a talent someone doesn't know they have and helping them to reach their true potential. Put people in roles where they will feel stretched.

— Zahra Bahrololoumi

Help your mentees develop and update their CVs. Often, people forget to include prizes they have won or achievements made.

— Frances Ruane

Take an interest in people. Give them the confidence to be open with you. Introduce them to new networks.

— Louise Richardson

Grease
the wheels
with effective
communication

Build shared values and articulate them in an accessible style.

— Brian MacCraith

Communicate well. If you are keen for a large audience to read your reports, make sure they are easy to read and understand. Stand up straight at the podium when you deliver a talk.

— Mary Kelly

Think about what motivates the person you are talking to.

— Mary Harney

We shouldn't just follow the narrative that is set for us. We need to listen carefully and challenge the language and words of the narrative more.

— Margaret Sweeney

Write down your thoughts on a situation, in work or out of it. Reflecting in this way helps you move on.

— Barbara Harvey

Determine who you need to speak with and work with to get things done. Draw the organisational chart if you are working with or in an organisation that has a complex hierarchy.

— Rhona Mahony

Laudable
leadership

Recognise your strengths. Work with others who can complement and support them.

— Rose Anne Kenny

Lead by example. Manage your time to avoid imposing on others. Set good precedents. Don't send emails late at night. Send them in the morning. Don't stay late in the office; others may feel they have to stay until you leave.

— Orlaigh Quinn

In leadership, people matter above all else. Listen to them. Show them they are valued.

— Brian MacCraith

The traits of leadership have traditionally been defined by men. We now need to have the confidence to redefine leadership in a less combative and adversarial style.

— Frances Fitzgerald

Loneliness can be a factor in leadership. Some people will desert you when the going gets tough. Be wary of those who are effusive in their praise. Avoid getting involved in idle gossip and backchat around you, or deflect it with humour.

— Rhona Mahony

Gestures matter as a leader.
Turning up to an event, a book launch or a funeral conveys respect and appreciation for the people involved.

— Brian MacCraith

You will rarely please everyone when making decisions. Take courses of action that are best for the organisation, rather than being best for you.

— Rhona Mahony

You can have a quiet leadership style. Use your influence for good. Leave something behind that's better than what you started with.

— Mary Kelly

Acknowledgements

This book would not exist without the wisdom, generosity and hard work of many people.

Thank you to all at Accenture and the Royal Irish Academy for supporting and organising the Women in Leadership Masterclasses, especially Dr Michelle D. Cullen, Pauline McNamara and Karen Muldowney. Special thanks also to Pauric Dempsey for his work on the original concept and his advice throughout.

Thank you to Ruth Hegarty at the Royal Irish Academy's Publications Office for the editorial vision and guidance in creating this short book.

Thank you to all the masterclass participants, who through their stories, questions and suggestions created an atmosphere of collegiality, inspiration, humour and learning.

And thank you, reader, for choosing to learn from others.